MATTHEW (POTTER) WOOD ON REDESDALE

Matthew Wood was born on 4th September 1919 at Silloans Farm, which h[...] become part of the Redesdale Artillery Range seven years earlier. His parents we[...] Matthew and Ciscilia Wood, who had three sons and four daughters. From an early ag[...] he was known as Potter, because an aunt had remarked that Matthew was alwa[...] pottering about. The name stuck! Now retired, Matthew Wood is the shepherd[...] shepherd. Few can even equal his knowledge of sheep. At the Upper Redesdale Show, h[...] won the championship cup for Blackface Sheep three times in succession and four time[...] in all. In memory of his father and uncle, he presented the Matthew Wood and John Scot[...] Memorial Challenge Cup for the Best North of England Blackface Sheep. He has lived in[...] three of the loveliest valleys in Northumberland – the Rede, the North Tyne and Tynedale, where, for thirty years, he ran Whitshields Farm, near Bardon Mill. However, he spent his first twenty years on Silloans Farm and he is a Redewater man, born and bred.

"The Reverend Thomas Newlands christened me and taught me the Gospel. Every Sunday, we would go to Sunday-school at Rochester Presbyterian Church. I started shepherding as soon as I left school at the age of fourteen. Every week, the Range Officer brought us a list to tell us when and where the firing was due to take place. During the summer months, when the troops were firing, we got up at four or half past four every morning and were away to the hills to get the sheep out of the way of the targets. Most of the firing took place around Silloans and towards East and West Wilkwood. We had to be back at Silloans by half past eight in the morning because the troops started firing at nine o'clock and we had to leave the house! The Army put up a tent for us about half a mile down the road towards the Sills Haugh. We could do nothing until they had finished firing because the shells came whizzing right over the top of the house. If the guns stopped firing, we would sometimes get the sheep out again in the afternoon.

My father came to Silloans from the Craig near Elsdon in 1887 when he was a year old. When Silloans was sold to the Army in March 1912, Robert Bruce rented the land and we became his shepherds. Robert Bruce came from a well known Border family, who had employed up to 40 Border shepherds on over 32,000 acres of land. He also had Carshope, where my uncle, Billy Hall, was his shepherd. I used to walk over by the Ridlees and Bygate Hall to take my holidays at Carshope. I would catch fish in the River Coquet, which flowed right past the door of the farmhouse!

I remember when an adder bit my father. He had been lying outside the tent, one July afternoon, waiting for the troops to finish firing. He had fallen asleep beside the wall when he felt something crawling over his face. He got up but the adder bit him on the wrist. We called Dr. Miller from Bellingham, who told my father to drink as much alcohol as possible: one poison would fight the other. My father drank almost a bottle of whisky. This saved his life but his arm swelled up and he spent a long time in hospital.

The roads were poor. The old Roman Dere Street went right up to Featherwood and a road branched off to Silloans. Apart from these, there were no proper roads, until they started to build the new roads for the heavy artillery. They built a big hut for 14 or 15 horses about 300 yards north of Silloans. The carters lived around this hut while they built the roads. Everything had to be done by horse and cart.

There was no electricity at Silloans – we used oil lamps. We got our water from a spring at the back of the house, near the burn, but in the early 1930s, they put water in from the main spring that supplied the whole camp at Rochester. It was between Silloans and Featherwood and was the best spring water that you would taste in your life!

Mother did all the cooking and baking and learnt to put up with the firing. The soldiers would often come for a glass of milk or something to eat. About twice a week, she would bake eleven or twelve loaves. We were self-sufficient in most things but at the back end of the year we would go over to Fodderlee on the Scotch side. We took a couple of carts to pick up the provisions to last us over the winter, such as flour and potatoes.

SILLOANS Built in 1820 beside a rippling waterfall of the Sills Burn, Silloans Farm was the home of Matthew and Ciscilia Wood and their seven children. Ivie Murray from Barrowburn had Silloans Cottage on the right until the sons of Matthew and Ciscilia were old enough to help with the shepherding. Many farms had tied cottages for their hired labour to help with the running of a 3,500-acre farm like Silloans. The limited opportunities for boys and girls after they left school meant that the boys often worked as farm hands and the girls went into domestic service. The family left Silloans in 1939 when the sons were called up for army service. Matthew could not manage such a large farm by himself and so moved down to the smaller farm of East Highridge, between Wark and Bellingham.

3

WOOD FAMILY PORTRAIT   W. P. Collier was often asked to take special pictures and family portraits and he made several visits over the years to Silloans Farm, the home of Matthew and Ciscilia Wood and their family. This picture was one of several taken in 1927, four years before the birth of Margaret, the youngest of the four sisters. Mother and father are surrounded by their children. Matthew (Potter) Wood stands on the left and Jessie sits on the lap of her mother. Robina leans on the knee of her father. Behind her stands John, the eldest of the three brothers, and next to him is Alec. Jane, the eldest sister, stands on the right. The whole family has dressed up for this charming portrait, which was taken outside the farmhouse door, with the farm peat stack visible in the top left-hand corner.

The next farm to us was Featherwood, which was often affected by firing more than we were because some of the targets were very near the farmhouse. This was the farm of Jack Carruthers, who was a great sheep clipper. And so was my father, who would win the clipping competition at the Rochester Show more times than anybody else. If any sheep had to be taken to a show, Jack Carruthers or my father would do the clipping. The youngsters would clip the draft ewes before they were sent to market. Everything had to be done properly. It was a sort of passing-out ceremony for the young shepherds to clip the draft ewes. This is where I learnt the skills of clipping!

All the farms would get together for the annual sheep clipping, which would take a fortnight or more. We would go with Featherwood, Stewart Shiels, the Dudlees, Branshaw, Yatesfield, the Wilkwoods and the other local farms. It always took two or three days to clip at Silloans, though most of the places around would take one day. There were always twelve or fourteen clippers. One man would wrap the fleeces into sheets; another would put a bit of tar on the wound, if one of the clippers nicked a sheep. I marked the sheep with a mixture of tar and pitch. Stewart Shiels had an S, Tofthouse had a T, the Dudlees had a D but Robert Bruce, who had Silloans and many other farms, had a distinct mark of his own in the shape of a cross. The clippers always finished at Silloans on the Friday night before the Jedburgh Games, one of the biggest athletic meetings in the country at that time. The young fellows would go to the Games the next day. After our sheep were clipped, we usually had three wagonloads of fleeces, which would be taken away to the woollen mills at Hawick.

Every year, Robert Bruce sent a man round all of his farms to buy the wedder lambs privately. We drove the draft ewes to Robert Donkin & Son, the auctioneers at Rothbury. This took two or three days. On the first day, we went to Davyshiel. The next day, we got to the Grasslees. On the third day, we arrived at the old racecourse at Rothbury. The other farmers would drive their sheep by the Rooken, Blackburnhead, and Emblehope over to Falstone station, where they put them on a train for Bellingham.

Silloans has always been one of the best sheep farms in Redewater. We had about 1,700 Blackface sheep on three or four thousand acres. Two of the biggest hirsels in Redewater were at Birdhopecraig and Harden Edge on Cottonshope. There were hirsels at Black Burn, the Sills, and the Rigg, which was the smallest hirsel.

Every summer, the Army staged a dog trial for the shepherds on the Range. It was the high point of the year and between thirty and forty people took part. All of the farms had collie dogs and Silloans had about ten. The Army collected everyone in their wagons and took them home again. They had a big marquee on the open fell just east of the hospital, near the Flagpole Ridge. The judge was always William Wallace of East Otterburn Farm, who was a great breeder of collie dogs. In 1938, I won the dog trial with Jean, who was the best collie that I ever had and she came from him! These trials stopped at the start of the Second World War and were never started again.

There were one or two dances in the wintertime at Rochester and Otterburn and two large dances a year were held in the big house at Catcleugh Reservoir for the Royal Victoria Infirmary. In addition to hunting and dancing, which were both great social events, people would go around the neighbouring farms for whist drives, music, or dances after the clipping. The farmers did not go down to the pubs very much. It was too far to go and they organised their own entertainment. All the farmers played quoits. Matches took place in the evenings or on social occasions and during the clippings – but it was often hard to get back to work after a good game of quoits!

I remember one April day when Mr. Collier came to Silloans on his motorcycle, with his camera and tripod strapped on his back. He took one picture of the house and others of the whole family sitting at the end of the house. Father and mother sat together and all of the children sat around them, with the youngest on mother's knee.

The Rede Valley is a special place because it reminds me of my shepherding days at Silloans, hunting with the Border Foxhounds, and looking out over the tremendous expanse of open country from my favourite spot at Ridlees Cairn!"

REEDSMOUTH.

234.

REEDSMOUTH   Local children gather outside the stationmaster's house, the most imposing of the 10 houses built in brick for railway staff. To the rear was the corrugated iron Railway Mission Hall, opened on 20th November 1897 to mark the diamond jubilee of Queen Victoria. Fifteen miles from Hexham and two miles from Bellingham, Reedsmouth (the traditional spelling used by the North British Railway) was named after the confluence of the Rede and the North Tyne, a short distance from Reedsmouth Hall, which dates from the 16th century. The Border Counties line opened in 1862 and ran 42 miles from Hexham to Riccarton Junction. Reedsmouth became a true railway junction in 1865 with the opening of the Wansbeck line, which ran 25 miles from Morpeth to Reedsmouth.

REEDSMOUTH The Border Counties line to Riccarton Junction goes to the left and the Wansbeck line to Morpeth via Scotsgap passes under the bridge on the right. The 1936 passenger timetable advertised six weekday trains between Hexham and Riccarton Junction and four between Reedsmouth and Scotsgap, where connecting services ran to Morpeth and Rothbury. Extra trains ran on Tuesdays and Saturdays and for important events like the Bellingham Show and the Bellingham lamb sales. Children from Bellingham would often travel to Reedsmouth station to watch the trains, paying a ½d. for the four-minute journey and crossing the River Rede 50 feet below on the magnificent skew-arch Reedsmouth viaduct, with its five spans and double width embankments.

REEDSMOUTH

REEDSMOUTH   The Wansbeck line closed to passengers on 13th September 1952, followed by the Border Counties line on 15th October 1956. Goods services and excursion trains continued for some years but the entire system had closed by 3rd October 1966. The station building had become a private house by 1979. A modern slate roof replaced the huge water tank, made at the Hexham Foundry of Thomas Davison, which weighed 100 tons and was supported on massive stone walls and heavy steel joists. The signal box was later converted into a house. The engine shed now contains 80 cubicles for cattle. The nearest building to the station was the little wooden shop of Florence Scott, where the local children would stop to buy sweets for their journey to and from school in Bellingham.

RIDSDALE   The importance of this iron-making village peaked in 1846 when Ridsdale iron accounted for almost one-fifth of the 5,050 tons of metal used in building the High Level Bridge in Newcastle. By 1849, economic factors had brought iron making to an end. In 1864, Sir William Armstrong bought the whole of Ridsdale and resumed the manufacture of iron for use in his Elswick armaments works. The village survived the closure of the ironworks in 1880 and the castle-like structure of the engine house still remains. The nearest of the buildings on the left was Ridsdale School, which closed in 1946, and the furthest housed the business of John Nesbit, the village butcher, who helped his mother to run the Armstrong Arms, the village local, which is now called the Gun Inn.

RIDSDALE Children stand outside Ridsdale shop and post office, which closed in November 1992, after being in the Slassor family for at least three generations. Half a mile down the hill, at the junction of the road to Knowesgate and Kirkwhelpington, was Sarelaw, the shop of Matthew Graham (1857-1918), whose wife Mary was a member of the Slassor family. This respected tradesman had a storehouse and wooden shop at Woodburn station, another large shop in Rochester and (until 1916) another outlet in the isolated colliery village of Plashetts. Following his motto *Supply a customer even should the transaction inconvenience yourself,* this familiar figure travelled the roads from Reedsmouth to Reidswire, even selling on one occasion the coat off his own back to a workman at Catcleugh Reservoir.

WEST WOODBURN   Woodburn station was situated on elevated ground ¾-mile south of the village. The station was typical of the six local stations on the Wansbeck line between Reedsmouth and Morpeth. A signal box controlled a passing loop and sidings. A heavy crane and loading ramp offered good facilities for freight and livestock. Large concrete letters spelled out Woodburn on the bank opposite the station platform. This station was an important disembarkation point for troops, horses and military equipment destined for the Redesdale Artillery Camp. The Wansbeck Piper was the last excursion train to visit Woodburn on 2nd October 1966. The large building behind the signal box was the storehouse of Matthew Graham. His wooden shop is hidden behind the station.

WEST WOODBURN Standing by the River Rede, the Bay Horse Inn is still known as the Bridge End. The lintel over the door bears the date 1797. The sign proclaims the tenancy of John Sisterson, dating this picture to around 1914, forty years before Rose Cottage, on the right, which was originally the house of the landlord, was converted into a kitchen and letting bedrooms to become part of the enlarged public house. The school and Methodist Chapel complete the row of buildings on the right, which included the shop of Ralph Charlton, the local butcher, the grocery shop of Thomas Simpson and the post office of Ernest Pigg. The village had a dressmaker, two banks, which opened on either Thursday or Friday afternoons, and James Hedley, the village carpenter and undertaker.

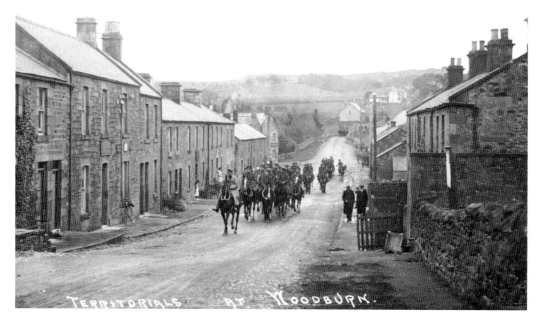

TERRITORIALS AT WOODBURN.

TERRITORIALS Woodburn station was an important disembarkation point for soldiers sent to train at the Redesdale Artillery Camp. Propping his bicycle against West Woodburn shop and post office, which was run for many years by the Pigg family, W. P. Collier took several pictures of the men as they began their 10-mile route march from West Woodburn to Rochester. A few residents stand along the road to witness one group of soldiers while another group is crossing the River Rede on the hump-backed bridge. This was rebuilt in 1957. The Presbyterian Chapel, which was built in 1894, can be seen beyond the bridge. On Brandy Bank in the far distance is the Fox and Hounds public house. Economics had forced this once-busy roadside inn, opposite the old smithy, to close by January 2000.

PEACE CELEBRATIONS   Saturday 19th July 1919 was kept as a National Holiday to celebrate the signing of Peace with Germany. The celebrations at West Woodburn were organised by Ernest Pigg M.M. (1884-1921) and held in a field lent by Mr. Robson of Chesterhope. At 1.30, the local schoolchildren met at Woodburn station and were escorted to the field, where Mrs. Purdie of Lowlands presented souvenir beakers. The men of East Woodburn won the sports competition. The children of Corsenside School performed their maypole dance under the supervision of Frederick Alvey, who was headmaster from 1910 to 1942, and his wife Lucy, who taught the infants. The celebrations finished at 10 o'clock with the presentation of prizes to both children and adults in the Village Institute.

OTTERBURN MILL A fulling mill had stood on the Otter Burn from the late 13th century but Otterburn Mill was founded in 1821, when William Waddell took over the *Little Old Mill* and began the manufacture of tweeds, blankets and travelling rugs. The long building was the machine weaving room, in front of which blanket cloth can be seen hanging on the long, wooden tenter frames. The washed cloth was hooked onto the upper and lower rails of tenterhooks. The heavy lower rail of hooks was then released and pegged down to stretch the cloth as it dried in the sun and wind before further processing. These are probably the last remaining tenter frames in the world and date back to the early 18th century. This method of stretching cloth has led to the expression *being on tenterhooks.*

OTTERBURN MILL The ground floor of the tall building on the left housed the carding and blanket machines. Hand weaving was done in the upper storeys. The Waddell family lived in the house behind the tree. The showroom, built in 1928, was on the far right. Otterburn Mill was perhaps most famous for its Pram Rug but had an equally high reputation for supplying quality tweeds to the fashion market. In 1976, inflation and competition from foreign imports forced John Waddell to close the Mill. In 1995, the Mill passed into the hands of the Pringle family, who have created an industrial museum and visitor centre. The old machine weaving room has become a large Mill shop and showroom. Many items of machinery and equipment from the old Otterburn Mill are on display.

BUNGALOW CAFÉ *Luncheons, Teas, High-class catering. Everything of the Best. All cakes and pastries are made on the premises. Delicious pastries and confectionery. Fresh country eggs always in stock. You are assured of a good meal at all times! Mineral Waters. Confectionery. Best makes always in stock. Parties catered for.* This advertisement shows that the Bungalow Café was already a thriving business, standing on the major coach routes, when Kate and John Jackson took over from Robert and Eleanor Telfer in the late 1920s. Kate was a shrewd shopkeeper and John delivered bread and cakes in his van. The couple bought the Carter Cottages and Café when the Otterburn Tower Estate was sold in 1931, replacing the wooden Bungalow in 1937 with the Carter Café, now the Border Reiver coffee house and village shop.

OTTERBURN A boy stands outside Carter Cottages, two of which face the main road and two face the road to Bellingham. These four cottages were built in the middle of the 19th century for the employees of Otterburn Tower, which from 1905-1928 was the home of wealthy author and historian Howard Pease (1863-1928) and his wife Marna. In the corner house lived the talented head gardener to Howard Pease, George McDougal, who for over 30 years took meticulous care in maintaining the grounds of the 90-acre Tower Estate. These included two Victorian walled gardens, a large heated glasshouse for growing peaches and grapes, ornamental gardens and woodland walks. In the cottage nearest to Otterburn Mill lived the Redewater policeman, who had the village lock-up in his house.

19

OTTERBURN The large building behind the Bungalow Café and the arched stables of East Otterburn Farm was the Presbyterian Manse. It was converted from a combined church and manse, dating from 1835, when the new Presbyterian Church opened beside it on 21st January 1884. A large fire was always needed to heat this rambling building and the north-facing side, which housed the domestic staff, was particularly miserable because it never received any direct sunlight except for a few weeks in the summer. The minister and his wife lived on the south side. The Manse was demolished in the 1960s because the Church found it difficult to maintain such a large dwelling. The roof of the old United Methodist Church, built in 1909, can just be seen in the distance.

OTTERBURN TOWERS   484.

OTTERBURN TOWER   The original Pele tower was built by the Umfraville family and is mentioned in the Battle of Otterburn. The tower passed to the Hall family but was confiscated when "Mad Jack Hall" was hanged for his part in the Jacobite Rebellion of 1715. Extensions were added by Reynald Hall of Catcleugh, Thomas James of Rutchester, who created the Gothic appearance and, in the early 20th century, by Howard Pease. Otterburn Tower had two owners after the sale of the Tower Estate in 1931 before opening as a hotel under Hugh Holliday in 1944. Its popularity grew under Major William Henderson. With its painted frieze of the Battle of Otterburn, stained glass windows and fine oak panelling, Otterburn Tower reopened in June 1999 as a country hotel and restaurant.

OTTERBURN This view of the 1930s depicts two busy garages, each competing with a fine display of advertisements and petrol pumps to cater for the increasing numbers of motor cars. Between them stands the former shop of Margaret Mitchell, just taken over by Lizzie Shanks. The further garage was started by Joseph Foster, who ran a local bus service and had cars for hire. He traded as Joseph Foster & Son when his son Gordon took over and then his grandson Kenneth. Thomas Gibson started the nearer garage, which John William Reed took over in 1927. He sold petrol in two-gallon cans and had the only cattle van in Redewater – until Joseph Foster got one. In time, Mick and Arthur Reed, the sons of John Reed, took over both of the garages but sadly both ceased trading in the late 1980s.

MURRAY ARMS In May 1855, John Snaith took over as landlord of the Percy Arms from Robert Anderson. The name of the inn was later changed in honour of Lord James Murray of Otterburn Hall. On the death of her father in 1877, Isabella Snaith took over the tenancy and bought the hotel when the Otterburn Hall Estate was sold in 1920. This respected lady served for over 50 years and died aged 86 in March 1927. The curving wall on the right separated the hotel from the gardens of the three adjoining private cottages. The small plaque to the left of the drainpipe records the Great Flood of Sunday 9th June 1907, when the Otter Burn burst its banks, flooding the village of Otterburn and submerging all the fine furniture and fittings of the Murray Arms to a depth of four or five feet.

PERCY ARMS HOTEL. OTTERBURN NORTH⁰

PERCY ARMS   *Many thousands of pounds, wisely spent in the successful attainment of an atmosphere that breathes quality, comfort and hospitality, should put the Percy Arms on the top line.* The death of Miss Snaith brought changes to the Murray Arms, which now reverted to the Percy Arms under its new owners, John and Jane Hodgson. By 1936, the conversion of the three cottages on the right had doubled the size of the hotel to 25 bedrooms and their gardens had become a new car park. The gleaming line of saloon cars reflects the advances made in motoring over 25 years and the popularity of the Percy Arms. Regulars came from Newcastle every weekend and competition was particularly fierce to stay over Christmas, when each guest would receive a present from under the large hotel Christmas tree.

OTTERBURN *M. Mitchell. Proprietors: Douglas and Robson. General dealers in groceries and draperies, confectionery, fancy goods, crest china, all kinds of stationery, local picture post cards; licensed to sell tobacco.* The long-established business of Margaret Mitchell was continued by two of her nieces for over 25 years after her death in 1907. Margaret Douglas is on the left and on the right is Anna Maria Douglas, who was the wife of Thomas Robson in the middle. This *dapper little fellow* worked in the offices of Otterburn Mill and was one of the Elders of the Presbyterian Church. The three lived together over the shop and are buried together with Margaret Mitchell in Otterburn Churchyard. The shiny brass plaque names the North Eastern Banking Company, which opened every Thursday in the front parlour.

OTTERBURN   This picture of Otterburn post office shows Mary Potts, the sub-postmistress, and her husband James Potts. Stanley Potts, their son, became the sub-postmaster on the death of his mother in 1923. He left Otterburn with his wife Emma and young daughter around 1933. The post office housed the local telephone exchange. After Stanley Potts left, Kate Jackson ran the post office and Bungalow Café for a short time until Lizzie Shanks, the wife of retired Bellingham police sergeant Robert Shanks, established the post office in the village shop, which she had bought from the nieces of Margaret Mitchell. The brass plaque names Bellingham doctor James Graham Miller, who held his surgery in a room every Tuesday. The local branch of Lloyds Bank opened every Friday.

LUKE'S CAFÉ   After the departure of Stanley Potts and his family, Robert and Jane Luke bought the old post office building and opened a café and sweet shop. Afternoon tea was an important part of a day out and the café occupied a prime position for visitors to Redesdale! Robert Luke was a professional driver for Joseph Foster. "Granny" Luke was a very refined lady with high standards and a great sense of humour. She knew what her customers liked and stocked accordingly. Many of the local lads would buy sweets from her on Sunday night for their sweethearts, waiting for them on the seat under the big tree outside the shop. The message on the back of this postcard, dated August 1936, describes Jane Luke as *a sweet old lady, who keeps the village store and sells gorgeous black bullets.*

OTTERBURN WAR MEMORIAL.

VILLAGE HALL The Duke of Northumberland opened the War Memorial Hall on 3rd May 1923, remarking that no one would make the mistake of believing that the world had become an easier and safer place to live in than it was in 1914. Local subscription had raised £1,200 for the Hall, which was built of local stone and had seats for 240 people, together with a recreation and billiard room. An inscription over the entrance has the names of nine local men who died in the First World War. The plaques on either side record the names of almost fifty men who served and returned. The hall replaced an earlier structure, opened in January 1905, which had been one of the wooden huts used at Catcleugh Reservoir. The wall of the Miniature Rifle Range, opened in 1908, can be seen on the far left.

OTTERBURN CHURCH

OTTERBURN CHURCH The parish church of St. John the Evangelist cost £3,000 and was dedicated by the Lord Bishop of Durham on 27th October 1857. The architect was John Dobson, who was responsible for designing many of the finest streets and buildings in Newcastle on Tyne, including the High Level Bridge, Central Railway Station and many churches. On the right of the church steps is the grave of Evelyn Foster, eldest daughter of local garage owner Joseph Foster. On the night of 6th January 1931, she was found lying beside her hire car near Ottercops, having suffered such serious burns that she died a few hours later. The circumstances of her tragic death at the age of 28 still remain a profound mystery. The male passenger, whom she was driving to Ponteland, was never found.

OTTERBURN HALL HOTEL. 488.

OTTERBURN HALL   This red brick Victorian mansion, built by Lord James Murray in 1870, became the home of Sir Charles and Lady Louisa Morrison-Bell, until the 5,960-acre Otterburn Hall Estate was put up for sale on 15th July 1920. The Hall remained unsold until November 1922, when a Newcastle business syndicate bought it for conversion into a country hotel. Progress was beset with difficulties and rebuilding followed a major fire in 1930. The final feature to be added was the large glass conservatory, where the ladies ate sandwiches while their husbands played golf on the 18-hole championship course. From 1932, it could be said that the Otterburn Hall Hotel had *all the atmosphere and comfort of an English home plus a choice of indoor and outdoor sports and amusements that must be unique.*

Capt. Dawes Bi-Plane
Visit to Otterburn Hall
Oct. 25-27 1913.

CAPTAIN DAWES Flying at an altitude of 5,000 feet from York to Montrose in his army Maurice Farman biplane, Captain G. W. Dawes of the Royal Flying Corps caused great excitement when he landed at Otterburn Hall to spend the weekend with his aunt, Lady Louisa Morrison-Bell. The biplane attracted great curiosity among the locals, including Joseph Foster, on the left, who stops his four-year-old daughter Dorothy from getting too close to the machine. Before leaving for Scotland on Monday, the gallant captain gave an exhibition flight for the children from Elsdon and Otterburn schools, at the invitation of Lady Louisa Morrison-Bell. W. P. Collier took a series of pictures of this unique event. The large writing and date confirm that this is one of his earliest known pictures.

"PERCY CROSS" OTTERBURN NORTH "WHERE DOUGLAS FELL 1388"

PERCY'S CROSS The Battle of Otterburn was fought on one moonlit night in early August 1388 between Scottish raiders, led by James, Earl of Douglas, and an English force, commanded by Sir Henry Percy, nicknamed Hotspur because of his impetuous nature. Percy was captured but Douglas was killed, the exact spot where he fell being marked by the so-called Battle Stone. During the construction of the Elsdon and Reedwater Turnpike road, which began in 1776, the socket that held the Battle Stone was moved 150 yards to the south-west of its original site and cemented into the top of a new pedestal base. A stone lintel, said to have been taken from the kitchen fireplace at Otterburn Tower, was then dropped into the socket. It is possible that the stone lying in the porch of Otterburn Church is part of the original Battle Stone.

HORSLEY The nearest building was Horsley smithy, which had closed some years before W. P. Collier took this picture. Horsley was a busy place in the 18th and 19th centuries because it had facilities for both men and horses. The Redesdale Arms supplied fresh horses for stagecoaches and offered accommodation for travellers. The 1851 census records that the smithy employed four blacksmiths. Its most distinguished occupant was Edward Welton, who was a blacksmith for over 37 years and was widely known as the man who could repair anything. After his death on 18th February 1902, John Nevin had the business until the start of the First World War, when he moved to Otterburn. Fred Anderson, who was a motor and cycle agent, had the premises before opening his garage in Rochester.

REDESDALE ARMS   The Redesdale Arms, originally called Horsley Farm, is still known as the First and Last. Ben Prior, the landlord, stands proudly beside his new sign. Known as *the man who never forgot a face,* he enjoyed great popularity with both visitors and locals, who wrote a song, to the tune of Clementine, in his honour. Beer was served from the cellar in a large jug, covered with a cloth weighted down with heavy tassels. He died on 23rd April 1940 at the age of 67 years, after serving as landlord for 14 years. He was a noted breeder and judge of Hackney horses and was a member of Bellingham Rural Council. He is buried (with his wife Margaret) at Benton, where he had been stud groom to Mr. Eustace Smith for many years. *"What a character!"* are the words on the back of this postcard.

EVISTONES   Built in 1866 and enlarged in 1878, the former shooting lodge of Charles James (1st Lord Northbourne) looks down on Stobbs Farm, behind which the River Rede flows through a field called Gluttenshaugh. This was the home of the Rochester Picnic, renamed in 1927 the Upper Redesdale Show. A narrow swing bridge across the Rede gave pedestrian access. Animals and vehicles used the ford a short distance downriver. Several attempts were made to bridge the ford. In the Second World War, Canadian lumberjacks made a fine bridge out of logs but the Rede flooded and washed away their efforts. After the War, Christopher James (5th Lord Northbourne) built a new bridge with the help of the army and university students. This has been replaced by the present Bailey bridge.

ROCHESTER WAR MEMORIAL *"To the Glory of God and in proud memory of the men of this countryside who fell in the cause of right and freedom 1914-1918."* Situated opposite Rochester School, which closed in 1953, this fine war memorial records the names of 10 local men who fell fighting for their country and 44 others who returned. The local War Memorial Committee raised the total cost of £365.18.0d., which was a large amount for a small rural community. At the age of 42, W. P. Collier left Bellingham to serve as an aerial photographer in the Royal Flying Corps between July 1917 and March 1919. Little is known about his service life. He preferred not to talk about his experiences, though he admitted to letting the odd glass plate slip from his numbed fingers while in the air.

THE REDESDALE and OTTERBURN RANGES

Local tradition proudly maintains that it was Winston Churchill who conceived the idea of developing part of Upper Redesdale as an Artillery Practice Camp. This keen sportsman was a frequent shooting companion of the local aristocracy. In September 1900, he was a guest at Birdhopecraig Hall, the shooting lodge of Lord Redesdale. On this or a similar occasion, as he stood on what was later called the Flagpole Ridge and contemplated the vast expanse of moorland and lack of sport, he remarked that it could be better used for shooting guns than shooting game. From this casual remark, Upper Redesdale became the chosen site for the creation of a new Artillery Range.

Prompted by the findings of the various commissions that were appointed after the South African War to review the military capability of Great Britain, Richard Haldane, Secretary of State for War, created the Territorial Force, which came into being on 1st April 1908. Recognising the threat of a European War, he reorganised the Reserve system of the British Army and created an efficient fighting force by amalgamating a wide variety of local military organisations, such as the Yeomanry and Volunteers, which had often existed for hundreds of years. By 1912, his reforms had put more than 260,000 soldiers into the Territorial Force, which was known as the Territorial Army after 1921.

The Territorial Force was organised and equipped in the same way as the Regular Army but was based territorially so that local soldiers would train together in local units, which could reinforce the Regular Army. The increasing likelihood that this new band of volunteer soldiers would be deployed abroad demanded a change of strategy from fortress artillery to field artillery. The artillery batteries of the Territorial Army were equipped with field guns towed by horses and the soldiers needed extensive artillery ranges on which to practise manoeuvres. An annual 14-day period of intensive training was developed and this has remained a central feature of the Territorial Army.

The initial purchase of land by the War Office for the Royal Artillery Practice Camp took place in the twelve months between March 1911 and 1912. The original 19,000 acres included the farms of Carshope, Fulhope, the Ridlees, part of Blindburn, Linshiels, West Wilkwood, Bygate Hall, Makendon, Quickeningcote, Featherwood, Tofthouse, Windyhaugh, Pity Me, Birdhopecraig, Bellshiel, part of Stewart Shiels, Sills and Silloans. In March 1912, Birdhopecraig Hall was bought for use as a Senior Officers Mess.

Ambitious plans quickly followed to construct 50 miles of new road, much of it using the line of the Roman Dere Street, which ran from High Rochester to Chew Green. Two firms from Newcastle on Tyne were responsible for most of the work. George Simpson had the contract for the roads and Alex Pringle was responsible for erecting stables and other buildings. Telephone wires were laid and there was even a fleeting idea, never fulfilled, to resurrect the narrow-gauge railway from Woodburn station to Catcleugh, which had been built 20 years earlier for the construction of the Reservoir.

The Hexham Courant reported that firing was commenced for the first time on 11th June 1912, with about 1,000 officers and men encamped on the ground at Birdhopecraig. *Seen from the site of the old Roman Camp of Bremenium, this modern encampment has a most picturesque appearance, with its white tents on the broad expanse of moorland, backed in the distance by the Cheviots.* No military training took place in 1913 to allow further construction work to continue without interruption.

Soldiers of the Territorial Force came by special train to Woodburn station. Their 14-day period of intensive training under the supervision of the Regular Army began with a 10-mile route march to Rochester. The noise of wagons, gun carriages, horses and army boots could be heard for miles. As one West Woodburn resident observed, *about a hundred tons of hay have been unloaded and sheds, carts, motor lorries and Fodens have all been pressed into the business of transportation. Quite a bit of the road will have to be repaired.* (April 1917). Until the Second World War, an annual sheep-dog trial was organised for the shepherds on the Range, with plenty of ale and sandwiches to cement goodwill.

HIGH·ROCHESTER. REDEWATER. 445.

HIGH ROCHESTER The 5-acre Roman fort of Bremenium dates from the 1st century A.D. It became the most northerly occupied fort in the Roman Empire. The large rectangle of trees in the centre of this picture shows the line of the 3rd and 4th century ramparts and ditch, marked by the dips in the modern stone wall on the left. A medieval hamlet grew up within the Roman ramparts, using the stone from the abandoned fort. The old bastle house on the left has been modernised as a cottage. Behind the two-storey house on the right are the fine remains of the west gateway of the Roman fort. The stables of Redesdale Artillery Camp extend towards Birdhopecraig Hall on the far right. A series of stiles now gives access to the ramparts of Bremenium, which was excavated in 1852-3, 1855 and 1935.

HIGH ROCHESTER   The west gateway consists of a single portal that was recessed 7½ feet into the rampart and was flanked by towers some 13 feet broad. A modern wall blocks the rear. The lower courses were constructed with massive blocks of stone. The northern impost and its richly moulded cap and springer are still visible on the left. Even when the Romans had made Hadrian's Wall, 20 miles south, the permanent frontier, Bremenium continued to be occupied as an outpost fort. The west gateway overlooks the wide valley of the Sills Burn, which has seen military activity since Roman times. Modern artillery rumbles along the Roman Dere Street, which is flanked by the turf ramparts of eight Roman camps, most still clearly visible and carefully marked by star-topped metal posts.

HIPPERSON'S XI The melodeon and round plate give no clue as to why W. P. Collier took this picture of the men who built the Ranges. The foreman standing on the far left is probably Frederick Hipperson, who hailed from Newcastle on Tyne. Locals included Robert Nelson, the smart man on the far left kneeling, and Tom and Gilbert Waitt, two brothers, standing third and fourth from the left. The navvy standing on the right wears the customary heavy leather leggings tied with string below the knees. The Hexham Courant of 26th April 1913 reported that *the Government camping ground near Rochester again presents an animated appearance, due not to the military, as none are coming this year, but to the number of men at work road-making, draining and the erecting of shelters, stables, etc.*

REDESDALE ARTILLERY CAMP.

422

REDESDALE ARTILLERY CAMP This picture was taken near Hopesley House on what is now Bremenium Way. The old road to Silloans Farm, called the Bents Road, runs along the middle of the picture. Senior officers occupied Birdhopecraig Hall to the left of the long line of trees and the military hospital is the wooden hut to the right. Junior officers and other ranks lived in bell tents pitched near the lines of wooden shelters where their horses were stabled. This postcard was sent to Salisbury on 6th July 1914 at the height of the training season: *This is a photo of Redesdale Camp. We are a bit better now than when we came first. Please write soon.* For weary troops, who had limited time for writing, the postcard was ideal for letting people know that they were *all right and enjoying the scenery.*

SAUGHENSIDE REDEWATER.

SAUGHENSIDE Birdhopecraig farmhouse stands beside the new road to Birdhopecraig Hall. Bellshiel Farm is in the distance on the opposite side of the main road, which climbs over the slopes of Saughenside towards Byrness. The War Office bought Birdhopecraig Farm from Lord Redesdale in March 1912 and used the farmhouse and adjacent land to supply accommodation for the men engaged in building the many miles of new road required for the Artillery Range. Locals helped with the work but accommodation was limited and the troops lived under canvas. This postcard was sent to Hereford on 25th April 1914: *What price our camp! There are two tents behind the big one so you can see what a nice place it is when it rains (I don't think). I want you to look after this picture, as it is a good one.*

BIRDHOPECRAIG HALL It may well have been during a stay at this elevated shooting lodge that Winston Churchill made his legendary remark that the adjacent moorland would make an excellent Artillery Range. Senior Officers lived in the Hall while Junior Officers and other ranks were billeted in tents. In the 1930s, Michael Storey, who came from an established family of Elsdon stonemasons, built an extension, which was apparently the source of a fire that gutted the Hall on 20th August 1957. Firemen from Bellingham and Hexham could not contain the huge blaze, which ripped through the fine oak panelling and brought the roof crashing down. Salvers, spoons, knives and forks melted into a stream of silver. Firemen noted a stone inscribed J. Green 1827 in the smouldering debris.

REDESDALE ARTILLERY CAMP FROM OFFICERS' MESS 8.

REDESDALE ARTILLERY CAMP Demands made on the British Army during the early 20th century required the expansion of training facilities and many men thought that hard work was better rewarded in the army than on the farm or in the factory. With their rank pay, separation allowances, training bounty and camaraderie, many Territorials looked forward to their annual 14-day training camp. The drainage and road-making programme completed in 1913 had made Redesdale Camp a more comfortable place. There were shower and foot baths, drying rooms and a hospital. Hangars were erected for the use of aircraft. Wooden shelters with concrete floors could house more than 600 horses. The unlimited supply of manure available by the wagonload was a bonus for local farmers.

REDESDALE ARTILLERY CAMP.   12

REDESDALE ARTILLERY CAMP   Looking north-west along the Bellshiel road towards the hospital on the far left, this picture is dominated by the wooden stables for the horses and the tents for the troops. The tents were removed at the end of the training season but the stables, which were made of wood and corrugated iron sheets, remained all through the winter and were maintained by a battery of the Regular Army. Horses were usually hired from local suppliers but the Regular Army and the Territorials had some of their own. The soldiers took good care of the horses and fed them on the best hay available. Many found it hard to control the six or eight horses that were required to pull a gun carriage over boggy ground. There is little evidence that motorised transport was widely used until 1934.

MILITARY HOSPITAL REDESDALE ARTILLARY CAMP. 11.

MILITARY HOSPITAL The concrete foundations of the military hospital are still visible near the Bellshiel road about ¼-mile north of Birdhopecraig. Metal bolts secured the asbestos outer walls and the wooden inner panels. The main hospital building, 11½ metres long and 4 metres wide, had two fireplaces and could accommodate about six soldiers. Serious accidents were rare, though local shepherds marvelled at the casual way that the soldiers would collect unexploded shells, which had been marked with red flags, and throw them into their wagons to be taken away for disposal. More danger was likely to come from adders. Many soldiers saw the annual camp as the nearest thing that they would get to a holiday. Even a stay in the hospital meant an unlimited supply of tea and sandwiches.

"HEUL" REDEWATER.

HUEL W. P. Collier has walked up from Birdhopecraig Presbyterian Church along the old road to Silloans. The modern road past Birdhopecraig farmhouse and Redesdale Camp has superseded what was part of Roman Dere Street. The open land around Huel Crag was a favourite place for hunting, especially on New Year's Day, when smoke would be seen rising from the fires that the shepherds lit to keep foxes out of their earths. The Border Foxhounds would usually find a fox near the Sills Burn, in the middle of this picture. In the days of religious persecution, the Covenanters would meet for worship in secret places among the rocks and Huel (Holy) Crag was one of four local places where they could meet and worship in safety. A fir plantation now conceals the craggy contours of the Huel.

PITY ME As the need for artillery training grew towards the start of World War Two, this small farmstead, just off Dere Street, was cleared and used for target practice. The same thing happened to the farms of Ridleeshope, the Ridlees, Dykeham's Edge, East Wilkwood and West Wilkwood. The lady at the door is probably Lizzie Waitt, who was the last person to live in Pity Me. Some of the best gooseberries in Redesdale came from her garden. Every other day, she would walk a mile down the road to Silloans Farm to get her milk. She stayed on for a time after her husband died but later moved down to Birdhopecraig Lodge to live with her son, Gilbert, the foreman of Robert Luce, who lived in Birdhopecraig farmhouse and was in charge of the men who worked on the Artillery Range.

The years between 1914 and 1918 saw a period of intense training to prepare both artillery and infantry units for the war in France. A replica sector of trenches was cut into the boggy ground, one mile north of Silloans Farm, consisting of first line, communication and support trenches. The trenches are in a remarkable state of preservation and serve as a reminder of the conditions that the troops of the First World War had to face.

The return of peace restored the previous pattern of training, with Territorial Army batteries and regiments coming to Redesdale between Easter and October for their annual 14-day training camp under the supervision of the Regular Army. This period saw a change from horse-drawn to lorry-drawn guns. In 1934, a tank battalion from Catterick undertook a trial of the suitability of the training area for use by tracked vehicles. The boggy ground was too soft for such heavy vehicles and the experiment was not repeated. It was even rumoured that one tank sank and disappeared without trace!

The period between 1940 and 1943 saw the creation of the Royal Artillery Practice Camp at Otterburn and a massive expansion of training facilities. Land at Otterburn was requisitioned in 1940 and compulsorily purchased between 1942 and 1943. The purchase or requisition of additional land in Redesdale and Coquetdale added some 32,000 acres and included the farms of Branshaw, North Yardhope, South Yardhope, Cottonshope and Cottonshope Head, Batailshiel Haugh, Shillmoor, Wholehope, the Trows, Linbriggs, Blindburn, Potts Durtrees, Yatesfield, Headshope, Barrowburn and Lounges Knowe, Rowhope, Harbottle Crags, Dudlees and High Carrick. Land was also bought at Huel Kirk, Bellshiel, Laingshill, Barrow, Linshiels, West Wilkwood, East Wilkwood, Girsonfield Moor, Stewart Shiels, Davyshiel Common, Carlcroft, Dunns and Wainfordrigg.

The incorporation of Cottonshope and Cottonshope Head within the Redesdale Artillery Range prompted the building of a new road from Low Byrness by Italian and German prisoners of war. The men had a camp just south of Cottonshope Farm and left their initials on some of the concrete culverts. Basic rations were supplemented by a bit of sheep rustling and yodelling was used to warn of an approaching shepherd!

The Camp at Otterburn included a brick-built HQ building, Range Control, hospital, showers and toilets to serve tented and Nissen-hutted camps. The requisition and purchase of land had doubled the size of the Ranges and had created the Otterburn Impact Area and surrounding Dry Training Area. With the return of peace in 1945, the Ranges continued to be used by the Territorial Army from Easter to October. The guns and radio vehicles, based permanently at Otterburn, were used for training between spring and autumn and were maintained by permanent staff during the winter.

A further 5,100 acres of land were bought between 1951 and 1954 on the southern edge of the training area, including the farms of the Craig, Laingshill, Dunns, Raw, High Shaw, part of Colwellhill and Girsonfield, Barrow, Angryhaugh, Holystone Common, Grasslees, Woodhouses, Herdlaw Farm, Herdlaw House and land at Hollin Burn.

From 1969, the Otterburn All Arms Training Area was increasingly used for fire and manoeuvre training by infantry units supported by artillery, mortars, guided missiles and air to ground attack aircraft. Both Otterburn and Redesdale Camps were improved for all-year occupation. Otterburn is now the largest single firing range of the twelve Army Training Estates in the United Kingdom and offers live firing and other facilities for members of both the Regular and Territorial Army. The most recent acquisition was the purchase in 1987 of 1,400 acres of land at Stewartshiels Plantation and Shepherd's Crag, including land at Byrness Hill and part of Coldtown Farm.

The Otterburn Training Area now consists of 30 tenanted farms and over 57,000 acres, of which some 29,000 acres are set aside for non-firing training. It is the only place in the United Kingdom where the Army can train properly on its modern artillery systems. Strict guidelines are in place to promote the conservation of this huge estate and new initiatives are being developed to allow greater public access to this area of outstanding historical interest and natural beauty. Ironically, in order to maintain the highest standards of training, plans were published on 6th December 2002 to demolish the 90-year-old Redesdale Camp for development as a wooded battery echelon area.

ROCHESTER Members of the Leighton family watch a Vickers tank outside their home. The building with the porch was Rochester post office. Robert and Annie Leighton had five sons and three daughters, none of whom married. By 1906, Robert had combined his drapery business and general store with the post office, which he took over from Mary Potts (née Welton) when she succeeded Elizabeth Davidson as sub-postmistress at Otterburn. The shop was crammed full with goods and provisions. Mary, the eldest daughter, became sub-postmistress on the death of her father in 1917. Norman brought children to Rochester School in his car. Fred was the local postman. They were all very musical and sat together in the choir stalls at Horsley Church, where Mary was organist for over sixty years.

ROCHESTER Rochester Village Hall, on the right, was opened by Lady Redesdale on 11th August 1928. The local committee organised a bazaar and sports competition in the afternoon to raise funds for the building and a dance followed in the evening. Local dances and concerts, even the Hunt Ball, were often quite simple affairs but people looked forward to them for weeks. Those living on isolated farms would walk for miles. Families would arrive in the light at dusk, stay all night and leave in the light at dawn, having had their fill of singing, dancing and playing on the fiddle and Northumbrian pipes. Rochester garage, run for many years by Fred Anderson, is just visible behind the Village Hall. Motorists of the 1920s had to plan their journey carefully to avoid running out of petrol.

THOMAS NEWLANDS No one could mistake the white beard of the Reverend Thomas Newlands, wearing his flat hat, which he tied over his head with string in windy weather. He served at Birdhopecraig Presbyterian Church between 1875 and 1931, usually walking to the isolated farms or riding on his bicycle or pony. The son of a Banffshire crofter, this generous and greatly respected minister died on 24th July 1932 in his 90th year. He could speak eight languages and recite much of the Bible from memory. He would play the organ (and fiddle) with the two good fingers on his right hand and lead the singing, if the congregation was a *wee bit thin*. This "Shepherd of the Hills" served the people of Redewater with deep devotion and the local children were often named Newlands after him.

BIRDHOPECRAIG CHURCH and MANSE   REDEWATER   482.

BIRDHOPECRAIG CHURCH   The bridge over the Sills Burn was widened in 1962 to incorporate the 30-inch diameter pipeline from Catcleugh Reservoir. On the right is Birdhopecraig Presbyterian Church, built in 1826 to accommodate 450 people. Redesdale has always been strongly non-conformist with an element of Scottish dissenters. The church was described as being well attended considering the thinness of the population. The Manse to the left was built by the congregation in 1876 at a cost of £900. The building behind the church was called the Common Stable, long demolished, where people would leave their horses when attending services and from where they could collect their groceries, when firing prevented local carriers from travelling to farms on the Artillery Range.

ROCHESTER, REDEWATER, NORTH. 504.

ROCHESTER   Trees along both banks of the River Rede now obscure this view of Birdhopecraig Manse and the west side of the village. The old road to Silloans Farm can be seen on the far left of this picture, which was taken from the field of Rochester Football Club. The Royal Electrical and Mechanical Engineers replaced the old wooden bridge across the Rede, known locally as the shaky bridge, by a suspension bridge in 1942 so that troops could use the field for football matches. Robert and Lily Nelson lived in the bungalow next to the Manse. Robert worked on the Range and Lily opened a tearoom and baked her own bread and cakes. This was a favourite rendezvous with soldiers and cyclists: twenty or thirty cycles could often be seen propped against the fence in the summer months.

BLAKEHOPEBURNHAUGH · REDEWATER, NORTH⁰ · 540.

BLAKEHOPEBURNHAUGH The Pennine Way here follows the old drove road, which connected the Rede and North Tyne Valleys, and passes between the farmhouse on the left and the former shepherd's cottage on the right. Farmers would drive their sheep along this route to Falstone station or Bellingham market. Walkers from Bellingham have followed the exposed track over Padon Hill, crowned with a memorial to Alexander Peden, a Scottish Covenanter, and Brownrigg Head. The route enters Redesdale Forest at Rookengate and passes along Rooken Edge. Motorists can follow a Forest Drive, opened in July 1973, past Blackblakehope and Oh Me Edge to Kielder Castle. Those walking the Pennine Way will use their time in Redesdale to prepare for the final trek of 27 miles to Kirk Yetholm.

COTTONSHOPE BURNFOOT   REDEWATER   538

COTTONSHOPEBURNFOOT   The harsh climate of Redesdale made it vital for farms to be self-sufficient. The haystack supplied fodder for the animals and the kitchen garden provided potatoes and vegetables for the family. On the right, telegraph poles line the main road as it snakes its way to Byrness. The national shortage of timber after the First World War led to the creation of the Forestry Commission in 1919 and planting at Smales Farm in 1926 heralded the birth of Kielder Forest. Four years later, a similar plot of land was purchased in Upper Redesdale, where the cold climate, exposed position and wet soil suited trees like the Norway spruce, Scots pine, Japanese larch and Sitka spruce. The labour camp, opened in 1934 behind the farm, hastened the development of Redesdale Forest.

Byrness C.I.C.   Summer Camp.   507.

BYRNESS CAMP The response of the Labour government in 1929 to the rising tide of unemployment was to create 27 Instructional Centres, or labour camps, where the workless could learn the skills of the manual labourer. The unemployed attended for 12 weeks, living in wooden huts and working for up to nine hours a day for four shillings per week. Failure to attend the camp or complete the training meant the loss of dole money for their families. The remote locations of these camps meant that the Dolies, as they were called, had little chance to go far. The regime of these rehabilitation centres aimed to restore healthy minds and bodies. The conditions were tough and the men worked all day in constructing roads and drains for the new forests. They built this bridge across the River Rede in 1936.

BYRNESS PRACTICE CAMP. REDEWATER. 504

BYRNESS CAMP The permanent labour camp at Kielder opened in August 1933 for 140 unemployed men aged between 18 and 25. Wooden huts, washing facilities, canteen and workshops were grouped around a flagpole flying the Union Jack. Superior quarters for the instructors were placed some distance away. The manager was usually a retired Services officer. The summer camp at Byrness opened in 1934 to extend the training at Kielder. All camps were closed at the start of the Second World War and the records were destroyed. The stigma of these camps limited the number of postcards that W. P. Collier might hope to sell. Byrness became in turn a Prisoner of War camp and until 1984 a Forestry Commission outstation. The area was ultimately developed as the Border Park Caravan Site.

Low Byrness Redewater

LOW BYRNESS The further cottage was the home of William Bell (1862-1941) who was a lengthsman and maintained the stretch of road between Rochester and Carter Bar for 48 years until his retirement in 1933. As he walked the road each day, the "Bard of Rede" used his poetical skill and native talent to produce 362 poems, most of which were written between 1904 and 1907. One of his most famous poems "The Cleugh" appeared in the Hexham Courant on 17th December 1904 and was written in response to his being asked on a daily basis the way to Catcleugh Reservoir by individual men or families, who had been tramping along the road to find work. The nearer cottage was used as a post office for the local postmen, whose daily rounds included some of the most remote farms.

JACOB ROBSON   Jacob Robson was born at the Byrness in 1858 and was educated first at Byrness School, then at Jedburgh and finally at Merchiston Castle School, Edinburgh. He became Master of the Border Hunt in 1879 when John, his brother, married and moved to the Newton near Bellingham. He became tenant of the 3,000-acre Byrness Farm on the death of his father in 1881. "Old Jake" had a national reputation for breeding Blackface and Cheviot sheep and Highland cattle. He became the longest-serving Master of Foxhounds in England and, after completing 47 years in this office, he received in 1926 a life-size oil painting of himself from over 500 of his friends and supporters. He died in 1933 aged 75. The Border Foxhounds are said to have killed 5,000 foxes during his 54 years as Master.

BYRNESS On the right, the walled gardens of the Byrness extend down to the main road. For 60 years, this was the home of Jacob Robson. He ended his tenancy on 13th May 1918 and moved to Coldtown Farm near West Woodburn. The Byrness was put up for sale as *an important freehold Sheep and Cattle Farming and Sporting Estate of about 8,198 acres including the magnificent grouse moor known as Black Blakehope with Blakehopeburnhaugh and Hillhead, Byrness Raw, Byrness and Cottonshopeburnfoot.* The whole estate was bought by Sir James Marr, a wealthy Wearside industrialist, whose numerous chairmanships included the Sunderland ship builders, Sir James Laing & Sons. The Byrness became the first house in Redesdale to have electricity when Sir James installed a 24-volt ship's dynamo in one of the stables.

63

BYRNESS REDEWATER.

BYRNESS The tiny church of St. Francis is flanked on the left by the Rectory and on the right by the Byrness. After the death of Sir James Marr in 1932, the Forestry Commission bought almost 11,500 acres of land from his heirs, who took a 21-year lease on the Byrness and the fishing and sporting rights. The Byrness later became a private club for the forestry workers of the new village of Byrness, whose first occupants arrived in August 1953. The status of the Byrness as a hotel was confirmed when a full drinks licence was granted in 1959. It reverted to private ownership in 1987 and remains a welcoming hotel, conveniently placed alongside the Pennine Way and the Border Park Service Station, which opened in 1959. The original Byrness School, which closed in 1937, nestles beside the church.

CATCLEUGH FARM   REDEWATER   462.

CATCLEUGH   Catcleugh Farm overlooks Catcleugh Reservoir, which was planned in 1889 and constructed between 1894 and 1905 to secure a reliable water supply for the growing population of Tyneside, from where most of the workforce was recruited. Conditions were harsh and dangerous, as Catcleugh was hacked out of the hillside with picks and shovels. A new high-level road, two miles long, was built past Catcleugh Farm and Ramshope above the water level of the Reservoir. Chattlehope Farm was relocated and Catcleugh Lodge was submerged. Catcleugh was the home of Simon Dodd (1875-1949) who was one of the best known and respected of the Border sportsmen and farmers. From 1919, he was Joint Master of the Border Hunt with Jacob Robson, his brother-in-law.

CATCLEUGH Catcleugh Reservoir holds 2,305 million gallons of water and is two miles long. To the right are the three cottages, built in 1909 for resident workers. On the far right, Catcleugh House, which was built in 1893 for Charles Henzell, the Resident Engineer, stands on the old low-level road. It overlooked the huts built for the labourers. At times, over 600 men and their families were housed in two shanty towns, nicknamed Newcastle and Gateshead. Traders visited Catcleugh on Saturday and Thomas Newlands preached on Sunday. There was a licensed Canteen. A narrow-gauge railway brought building supplies from Woodburn station. A stained-glass window in Byrness Church was dedicated in 1903 to the 64 men, women and children who died during the construction of Catcleugh.

WHITELEE On the far right stands the last house in England, two miles from Carter Bar. The small dwelling, which existed in the late 17th century, developed into a substantial coaching inn, with the arrival of the Elsdon and Reedwater Turnpike road. On the far left, near the bridge over the Lumsdon Burn, stood a toll house, which was sold when tolls were abolished on 1st November 1880. A stone lintel over the original front door of Whitelee had the words *Pax sit huic domo intrantibus (Peace be to those entering this house)*. In December 1897, the Newcastle and Gateshead Water Company bought Whitelee, securing the streams that fed the River Rede and Catcleugh Reservoir and extending the house. Its function as an inn was superseded by the opening in September 1893 of the licensed Canteen at Catcleugh.

"CARTER BAR" CHEVIOT HILLS. 483

CARTER BAR   This was the end of the road for W. P. Collier, who produced no postcards of Scotland, except for a small set of pictures of Liddesdale. Standing on the English-Scottish Border, 418 metres above sea level, and overlooking the source of the River Rede, Carter Bar was the traditional meeting-place of the English and Scottish Wardens, who were chosen to arrange the arbitration of disputes and the exchange of prisoners. Two hundred metres to the east, a stone marks the site of one of the last Border fights, which occurred on 7th July 1575 and is related in the ballad *The Raid of the Reidswire.* It began with a friendly meeting between the Wardens and ended with the death or imprisonment of several English nobles. Only the prompt release of the English prisoners prevented an international incident.